Risotto Recipes

© Copyright 2018. Laura Sommers.
All rights reserved.
No part of this book may be reproduced in any form or by any electronic or mechanical means without written permission of the author. All text, illustrations and design are the exclusive property of
Laura Sommers

Introduction	1
Mushroom Risotto	2
Barley Mushroom Risotto	3
Bacon Risotto	4
Butternut Squash Risotto	5
Zucchini Risotto	6
Fennel Risotto	7
Spring Risotto	8
Spring Risotto	9
Lemony and Risotto	10
Chicken and Sausage Peppers Risotto	11
Shrimp and Arugula Risotto	12
Shiitake and Sweet Pea Risotto	13
Broken Spaghetti Risotto	14
Ham Risotto with Sugar Snap Peas	15
Cheesy Pumpkin Risotto	16
Bacon and Pine Nuts Pumpkin Risotto	17
Roast Pumpkin and Feta Risotto	18
Barley Risotto Primavera	19
Herb Barley Risotto with Peas and Arugula	20
Shrimp and Scallop Risotto	21
Risotto with Truffle and Parmesan	23

Green Risotto with Fava Beans 24

Farro Risotto 25

Italian Wedding Risotto Soup 26

Prawn and Pine Nut Risotto 27

Wild Risotto 28

Barley Risotto with Eggplant and Tomatoes 29

Gorgonzola and Wild Mushroom Risotto 30

Creamy Edamame Risotto 32

Sweet Pea Risotto 33

Creamy Quinoa Risotto 34

Lobster Risotto 35

Shrimp and Fennel Risotto 36

Chanterelle Mushroom Risotto 37

Creamy Corn Risotto 38

Cauliflower Risotto Cakes 39

Chicken Risotto 40

Risotto with Pesto 41

Risotto Milanese 42

Risotto Alle Vongole (Risotto with Clams) 43

Caramelized Carrot Risotto 44

Creamy Maple Bacon Pumpkin Risotto 45

Bacon, Cheddar & Beer Risotto 46

Red Wine Risotto 47

Caprese Risotto 48

Broccoli Cheddar Risotto 49

Spinach Basil Pesto Risotto 50

Crispy mozzarella risotto cakes 52

Seafood Risotto 53

Drunken Risotto with Spinach..54

Black Squid Ink Risotto..55

Creamy Maple Bacon Pumpkin Risotto........................57

Bacon, Cheddar & Beer Risotto 58

Red Wine Risotto 59

Caprese Risotto 60

Broccoli Cheddar Risotto 61

Spinach Basil Pesto Risotto 62

Crispy Mozzarella Risotto Cakes 64

Seafood Risotto 65

Drunken Risotto with Spinach..66

Black Squid Ink Risotto..67

About the Author 69

Other Books by Laura Sommers....................................70

Introduction

Risotto is the greatest thing to come out of Italy since pasta. Riso is "rice" in Italian and risotto is rice that has been cooked in broth until it is creamy. Although risotto is primarily a dish from Northern Italy, there are many modern variations of this tasty dish.

This cookbook contains many of the traditional risotto recipes as well as some delicious not so ordinary varieties. There are many great, easy to make mouth watering risotto recipes for you to try in this cookbook.

Mushroom Risotto

Ingredients:

6 cups chicken broth, divided
3 tbsps. olive oil, divided
1 pound portobello mushrooms, thinly sliced
1 pound white mushrooms, thinly sliced
2 shallots, diced
1 1/2 cups Arborio rice
1/2 cup dry white wine
Sea salt to taste
Freshly ground black pepper to taste
3 tbsps. finely chopped chives
4 tbsps. butter
1/3 cup freshly grated Parmesan cheese

Directions:

1. In a saucepan, warm the broth over low heat.
2. Warm 2 tbsps. olive oil in a large saucepan over medium-high heat.
3. Stir in the mushrooms, and cook until soft, about 3 minutes.
4. Remove mushrooms and their liquid, and set aside.
5. Add 1 tbsp. olive oil to skillet, and stir in the shallots.
6. Cook 1 minute.
7. Add rice, stirring to coat with oil, about 2 minutes. When the rice has taken on a pale, golden color, pour in wine, stirring constantly until the wine is fully absorbed.
8. Add 1/2 cup broth to the rice, and stir until the broth is absorbed.
9. Continue adding broth 1/2 cup at a time, stirring continuously, until the liquid is absorbed and the rice is al dente, about 15 to 20 minutes.
10. Remove from heat, and stir in mushrooms with their liquid, butter, chives, and parmesan.
11. Season with salt and pepper to taste.

Barley Mushroom Risotto

Ingredients:

5 cups chicken broth
1 tbsp. butter
1 onion, chopped
1 cup pearl barley
3/4 tsp. dried thyme
1 bay leaf
1 tbsp. olive oil
1 pound mushrooms, sliced
2 garlic, chopped
2 tbsps. chopped fresh parsley

Directions:

1. Bring chicken broth to a boil in a saucepan.
2. Melt butter in a large skillet over medium heat.
3. Add onion, and saute for 5 minutes.
4. Add the barley, thyme, bay leaf and 2 cups of the hot broth.
5. Bring to a boil, and reduce heat to low, and simmer until most of the broth is absorbed, about 10 minutes.
6. Pour in remaining broth 1/2 cup at a time, stirring and allowing it to become absorbed before adding more. This process takes about 50 minutes.
7. Meanwhile, heat olive oil in a large skillet. Saute mushrooms in the hot oil until tender.
8. Add garlic, and cook for about 3 more minutes.
9. Stir in the barley mixture and parsley.
10. Remove bay leaf, and serve.

Bacon Risotto

Ingredients:

1/2 pound bacon, diced
5 cups chicken stock
2 tbsps. butter
1/2 onion, diced
4 cloves garlic, minced
1 1/2 cups Arborio rice
2 tbsps. butter
1/4 cup grated Parmesan cheese
Salt and black pepper to taste

Directions:

1. Cook and stir the diced bacon in a large skillet over medium heat until browned, about 10 minutes.
2. Drain the bacon and reserve.
3. Bring the chicken stock to a boil in a saucepan over high heat; reduce heat to low to keep the chicken stock hot.
4. Heat 2 tbsps. butter in a large, heavy-bottomed saucepan over medium-high heat.
5. Add the onion and garlic; cook and stir until the onion begins to turn golden brown at the edges, about 2 minutes.
6. Pour in the rice and stir until the rice is coated in butter and has started to toast, 2 to 3 minutes.
7. Reduce heat to medium; stir in one-third of the hot chicken stock and continue stirring until the rice has absorbed the liquid and turned creamy.
8. Repeat this process twice more, stirring constantly.
9. Stirring in the broth should take 15 to 20 minutes in all. When finished, the rice should be tender, yet slightly firm.
10. Remove the risotto from the heat and stir in the remaining 2 tbsps. of butter, the Parmesan cheese, and the reserved bacon.
11. Season to taste with salt and pepper before serving.

Butternut Squash Risotto

Ingredients:

2 cups cubed butternut squash
2 tbsps. butter
1/2 onion, minced
1 cup Arborio rice
1/3 cup dry white wine
5 cups hot chicken stock
1/4 cup grated Parmesan cheese
Salt and ground black pepper to taste

Directions:

1. Place squash cubes into a steamer basket in a saucepan.
2. Add water, cover, and bring to a boil over medium-high heat. Allow to steam until the squash is tender (10 to 15 minutes), then drain, and mash in a bowl with a fork.
3. Melt butter in a saucepan over medium-high heat.
4. Add onion; cook and stir for 2 minutes until the onion begins to soften, then stir in the rice. Continue cooking and stirring until the rice is glossy from the butter, and the onion begins to brown on the edges, about 5 minutes more.
5. Pour in the white wine; cook, stirring constantly, until it has evaporated.
6. Stir in the mashed squash and 1/3 of the hot chicken stock; reduce heat to medium.
7. Cook and stir until the chicken stock has been absorbed by the rice, 5 to 7 minutes.
8. Add half of the remaining chicken stock, and continue stirring until it has been absorbed. Finally, pour in the remaining stock, and continue stirring until the risotto is creamy.
9. Finish by stirring in the Parmesan cheese, and seasoning to taste with salt and pepper.

Zucchini Risotto

Ingredients:

7 cups vegetable or chicken stock
1 tbsp. butter
1 medium onion, chopped
2 cups Arborio rice, uncooked
1/2 medium zucchini, thinly sliced
10 sun-dried tomatoes, softened and chopped
1 tsp. dried thyme, crushed
6 tbsps. freshly grated Parmesan cheese
1 tbsp. chopped fresh basil leaves
Freshly ground black pepper to taste

Directions:

1. Bring vegetable or chicken stock to a boil in a medium stock pot, then reduce heat to a low simmer.
2. Melt butter in a large, heavy bottomed stock pot over medium heat.
3. Stir in onions and cook for 2 minutes, or until softened.
4. Add the rice and cook for another 2 minutes, stirring constantly, until lightly toasted.
5. Gradually ladle in simmering vegetable stock, stirring continuously. Risotto will become "creamy" and slightly sticky, yet still firm in the center, or al dente.
6. When almost finished, stir in the zucchini, sun-dried tomatoes, and thyme, adding stock as needed and stirring continuously.
7. Stir in basil and 3 tbsps. cheese just before serving. Divide risotto among 6 bowls, sprinkle with remaining cheese, and season with pepper to taste.

Fennel Risotto

Ingredients:

4 bulbs fennel
1 tbsp. butter
1 medium onion, chopped
2 cups uncooked Arborio rice
7 cups vegetable broth
1 cup heavy cream
6 tbsps. freshly grated Parmesan cheese
1 tbsp. dried parsley
Freshly ground black pepper to taste

Directions:

1. Cut the base off of the fennel bulbs, and cut a cone shape into the base to remove the core.
2. Slice the fennel vertically (lengthwise) into 1/4 inch thick slices.
3. Melt butter in a heavy-bottomed stock pot over medium heat.
4. Cook onions and fennel in butter for 2 minutes.
5. Stir in the rice; cook for another 2 minutes, stirring constantly, until lightly toasted.
6. Stir in 1 cup vegetable broth; continue stirring until liquid is almost completely absorbed.
7. Repeat this process with remaining broth, stirring constantly. Incorporating the broth should take 15 to 20 minutes in all.
8. Stir in cream, 3 tbsps. Parmesan and parsley, and cook until rice is done and risotto is thick and creamy.
9. Season to taste with black pepper. Divide risotto among 6 bowls, and sprinkle with remaining cheese.

Spring Risotto

Ingredients:

3 tbsps. olive oil
3 tbsps. butter
1 bulb fennel, diced
1 small red bell pepper, diced
1 onion, diced
3 cloves garlic, minced
2 tsps. grated lemon zest
3 tbsps. chopped fresh mint leaves
3 tbsps. chopped fresh parsley
2 tbsps. chopped fresh rosemary (optional)
1/2 tsp. ground coriander
1 1/2 cups uncooked Arborio rice
1/2 cup dry white wine
3 1/2 cups hot vegetable stock
1 tbsp. fresh lemon juice, or to taste
1/3 cup grated Parmesan cheese
Salt and pepper to taste

Directions:

1. Heat oil and butter in a medium-size heavy saucepan over medium heat.
2. Stir in fennel, red pepper, onion, and garlic.
3. In a small bowl, mix together lemon zest, mint, parsley, and rosemary.
4. Stir half of this herb mixture into saucepan, and set the rest aside. Saute vegetables until slightly softened, 3 to 4 minutes.
5. Stir in coriander and rice.
6. Cook, stirring frequently, until rice grains are thoroughly coated with oil and butter.
7. Stir in wine, then reduce heat to low.
8. Stir in about 1 cup of vegetable broth. Continue to stir while ladling in more broth as needed; rice should have a thin veil of broth over it at all times.
9. Cook for 20 to 25 minutes, until all broth is used and absorbed, and rice is tender.
10. Remove pan from heat and stir in remaining herb mixture, lemon juice and Parmesan cheese.
11. Season to taste with salt and pepper.
12. Cover pan loosely with waxed paper and allow to stand 8 to 10 minutes before serving.

Spring Risotto

Ingredients:

3 tbsps. olive oil
3 tbsps. butter
1 bulb fennel, diced
1 small red bell pepper, diced
1 onion, diced
3 cloves garlic, minced
2 tsps. grated lemon zest
3 tbsps. chopped fresh mint leaves
3 tbsps. chopped fresh parsley
2 tbsps. chopped fresh rosemary
1/2 tsp. ground coriander
1 1/2 cups uncooked Arborio rice
1/2 cup dry white wine
3 1/2 cups hot vegetable stock
1 tbsp. fresh lemon juice, or to taste
1/3 cup grated Parmesan cheese
Salt and pepper to taste

Directions:

1. Heat oil and butter in a medium-size heavy saucepan over medium heat.
2. Stir in fennel, red pepper, onion, and garlic.
3. In a small bowl, mix together lemon zest, mint, parsley, and rosemary.
4. Stir half of this herb mixture into saucepan, and set the rest aside. Saute vegetables until slightly softened, 3 to 4 minutes.
5. Stir in coriander and rice.
6. Cook, stirring frequently, until rice grains are thoroughly coated with oil and butter.
7. Stir in wine, then reduce heat to low.
8. Stir in about 1 cup of vegetable broth. Continue to stir while ladling in more broth as needed; rice should have a thin veil of broth over it at all times.
9. Cook for 20 to 25 minutes, until all broth is used and absorbed, and rice is tender.
10. Remove pan from heat and stir in remaining herb mixture, lemon juice and Parmesan cheese.
11. Season to taste with salt and pepper.
12. Cover pan loosely with waxed paper and allow to stand 8 to 10 minutes before serving.

Lemony and Risotto

Ingredients:

5 tbsps. extra-virgin olive oil
2 tsps. kosher salt
1/2 tsp. freshly ground black pepper
1 pound extra-large shrimp, peeled and deveined
1 cup fennel bulb, chopped
1 cup onion, chopped
1 large clove garlic, smashed, peeled, chopped
1 cup Arborio rice
1/4 cup dry white wine
3 cups chicken broth, plus extra as needed
1/4 cup fresh lemon juice
Zest of 1 large lemon
3 cups arugula

Directions:

1. Heat 2 tbsps. of the oil in a heavy large saucepan over medium heat.
2. Add the shrimp and sprinkle with 1/2 tsp. of the salt and 1/4 tsp. of the pepper.
3. Cook until the shrimp are just opaque in the center, about 3 minutes.
4. Remove the pan from the heat. Transfer the shrimp and juices to a bowl to cool.
5. Add the remaining 3 tbsps. oil to the pan.
6. Add the fennel and onions.
7. Cook until tender, about 4 minutes.
8. Add the garlic and cook until aromatic, 30 seconds.
9. Add the rice.
10. Stir until well coated and translucent in spots, about 2 minutes.
11. Add the wine.
12. Cook until the wine is absorbed, stirring often, about 2 minutes.
13. Add the broth, lemon juice, zest, and the remaining 1 1/2 tsps. salt and 1/4 tsp. pepper. Increase the heat and bring to a boil, stirring often.
14. Reduce the heat to medium-low. Simmer until the rice is just tender but still has some bite and the risotto is creamy, stirring often, 13 to 14 minutes.
15. Mix in the arugula.
16. Stir until the arugula wilts, about 30 seconds.
17. Add the shrimp.
18. Mix in additional broth if needed, 1/4 cup at a time, until the risotto is creamy.
19. Spoon the risotto into 4 shallow soup bowls.

Chicken and Sausage Peppers Risotto

Ingredients:

6 bone-in chicken thighs with skin
1 tsp. salt
1 tsp. ground black pepper
2 tbsps. olive oil
1 pound linguica sausage, sliced
1/2 onion, chopped
1 tbsp. paprika
1 tbsp. ground cumin
1 tbsp. herbes de Provence
1 bay leaf
1 tsp. fresh parsley, chopped
4 cups chicken stock, or as needed
2 tbsps. olive oil
1 red bell pepper, chopped
1 mildly hot green pepper, such as a chilaca, chopped
8 oz. uncooked orzo pasta

Directions:

1. Season chicken thighs with salt and black pepper. Heat 2 tbsps. of olive oil on medium-high heat in a saucepan.
2. Cook chicken until browned, about 3-4 minutes on each side; remove from pan.
3. Cook and stir linguica sausage and onion in the same saucepan until the onion is just starting to become translucent, about 3 minutes.
4. Stir in paprika, cumin, herbes de Provence, bay leaf, and parsley; cook spices in oil until fragrant, about 3 minutes.
5. Return browned chicken thighs to the skillet, and pour in chicken stock.
6. Heat to a boil; reduce heat to low, and simmer, covered, for 30 minutes.
7. Remove all chicken pieces and sausage using a slotted spoon.
8. Pour broth into different bowl and set aside.
9. When chicken is cool enough to handle, remove skin and bones; set chicken meat and sausage aside.
10. Heat 2 more tbsps. of olive oil on medium heat in saucepan.
11. Add red and green peppers and orzo; stir to coat with hot oil.
12. Stir in 1-1/2 cups of hot broth, 1/2 cup at a time.
13. Cook for 5 minutes, or until most of broth is absorbed.
14. Continue to slowly add remaining broth and stir until almost absorbed, about 15 minutes, or until tender but still slightly firm in the center of a pasta (you probably won't use all of broth).
15. Remove from heat.
16. Add chicken and sausage, stir and cover. Let sit for 5 minutes, or until pasta soaks up remaining broth. You can pour in extra broth at serving time if mixture is a little dry.

Shrimp and Arugula Risotto

Ingredients:

4 cups chicken stock
2 tbsps. extra-virgin olive oil, divided
1 pound large shrimp, peeled and deveined
1/2 tsp. salt, divided
1/4 tsp. freshly ground black pepper, divided
1/2 cup chopped shallots
6 garlic cloves, minced
1 cup uncooked Carnaroli or Arborio rice
1/2 cup dry white wine
1/2 cup grated fresh Parmigiano-Reggiano cheese
2 tbsps. butter
3 cups baby arugula
1/2 cup thinly sliced fresh basil

Directions:

1. Bring chicken stock to a simmer in a small saucepan (do not boil).
2. Keep warm over low heat.
3. Heat 1 tbsp. oil in a large nonstick skillet over medium-high heat.
4. Sprinkle shrimp with 1/4 tsp. salt and 1/8 tsp. pepper.
5. Add shrimp to pan; cook 1 minute.
6. Remove pan from heat; set aside.
7. Heat remaining 1 tbsp. oil in a large saucepan over medium heat.
8. Add shallots and garlic to pan; cook 5 minutes or until tender, stirring frequently.
9. Add rice; cook 1 minute, stirring constantly.
10. Stir in wine; cook 1 minute or until the liquid is nearly absorbed, stirring constantly.
11. Add 1 cup stock; cook 4 minutes or until liquid is nearly absorbed, stirring constantly.
12. Stir in remaining stock, 1/2 cup at a time, stirring frequently until each portion of stock is absorbed before adding the next (about 25 minutes total).
13. Stir in shrimp; cook 1 minute or until done.
14. Stir in cheese, butter, remaining 1/4 tsp. salt, and remaining 1/8 tsp. pepper.
15. Remove from heat; stir in arugula and basil.

Shiitake and Sweet Pea Risotto

Ingredients:

4 cups chicken broth
1 tbsp. butter
1/2 cup finely chopped onion
1 1/2 tsps. minced garlic, divided
1 cup uncooked Arborio rice
1/2 cup dry white wine
1 tbsp. extra-virgin olive oil
4 cups thinly sliced shiitake mushroom caps
2 tsps. chopped fresh thyme, divided
3/4 cup frozen green peas
6 tbsps. grated fresh Parmigiano-Reggiano cheese, divided
1/4 tsp. freshly ground black pepper

Directions:

1. Bring broth to a simmer in a medium saucepan; keep warm over low heat.
2. Melt butter in a large skillet over medium heat.
3. Add onion; cook 2 minutes.
4. Add 1 tsp. garlic; cook 30 seconds, stirring constantly.
5. Add rice; cook 1 minute, stirring constantly.
6. Add wine; cook 2 minutes or until liquid is absorbed, stirring frequently.
7. Stir in 1/2 cup broth; cook 2 minutes or until liquid is absorbed, stirring constantly.
8. Add remaining broth, 1/2 cup at a time, stirring constantly until each portion of broth is absorbed before adding the next (about 20 minutes).
9. Heat oil in a large nonstick skillet over medium-high heat.
10. Add mushrooms to pan; sauté 5 minutes or until tender.
11. Add remaining 1/2 tsp. garlic and 1 tsp. thyme; sauté 1 minute. Set aside.
12. Stir mushrooms, remaining 1 tsp. thyme, peas, 1/4 cup cheese, and pepper into risotto; cook 3 minutes. Spoon about 1 1/4 cups risotto into each of 4 bowls; sprinkle each with 1 1/2 tsps. cheese.

Broken Spaghetti Risotto

Ingredients:

1 tbsp. olive oil
8 oz. uncooked spaghetti, broken into 1 inch pieces
2 cloves garlic, minced
1 1/2 cups chicken broth
1/2 tsp. red pepper flakes, or to taste
salt to taste
2 tbsps. freshly grated Parmigiano-Reggiano cheese
1 tbsp. chopped fresh flat-leaf parsley

Directions:

1. Heat oil in a saucepan over medium heat; add spaghetti and toast, stirring constantly, until golden brown, 3 to 5 minutes.
2. Stir garlic into spaghetti pieces and cook for 30 seconds.
3. Pour in 1/2 cup broth and increase heat to medium high.
4. Stir spaghetti and broth until all the liquid is absorbed, 2 to 3 minutes.
5. Repeat this process until all of the stock is absorbed and noodles are desired tenderness, about 10 minutes.
6. Reduce heat to low.
7. Season spaghetti with salt and red pepper flakes to taste.
8. Remove from heat.
9. Stir Parmigiano-Reggiano cheese and parsley into spaghetti and serve.

Ham Risotto with Sugar Snap Peas

Ingredients:

4 cups chicken broth
8 oz. sugar snap peas, trimmed and cut into pieces
2 tsps. olive oil
1 1/2 cups thinly sliced leek
2 garlic cloves, minced
1 cup uncooked Arborio rice
1/2 cup dry white wine
3/4 cup diced cooked ham
1/2 cup freshly grated Parmesan cheese
1/8 tsp. black pepper

Directions:

1. Bring broth to a simmer in a medium saucepan (do not boil). Keep warm.
2. Cook peas in boiling water 2 minutes or until crisp-tender.
3. Drain and rinse with cold water; drain.
4. Heat oil in a large saucepan over medium heat.
5. Add leek to pan; cook 5 minutes or until tender, stirring frequently.
6. Add garlic; cook 30 seconds.
7. Stir in rice; cook 1 minute.
8. Add wine; cook 2 minutes or until liquid is nearly absorbed, stirring constantly.
9. Add broth, 1/2 cup at a time, stirring constantly until each portion of broth is absorbed before adding the next (about 20 minutes total).
10. Add ham to pan; cook 3 minutes or until thoroughly heated.
11. Stir in peas, cheese, and pepper.

Cheesy Pumpkin Risotto

Ingredients:

2 tbsps. butter
1 cup chopped sweet onion
3/4 cup Arborio rice
1/2 cup Sauvignon Blanc wine
4 cups simmering hot chicken broth, divided
1/2 cup canned pumpkin puree
1/2 cup grated Gruyere cheese
1/4 cup grated Parmesan cheese
1/4 tsp. ground nutmeg
1/4 tsp. cayenne pepper
Fresh ground black pepper to taste

Directions:

1. Melt butter in a large saucepan over medium-high heat.
2. Saute sweet onion in melted butter until soft and translucent, 5 to 7 minutes; add rice and continue to cook, stirring frequently, until fragrant, about 2 minutes more.
3. Pour Sauvignon Blanc over the rice mixture; cook, stirring frequently, until the rice has absorbed the wine, 5 to 7 minutes.
4. Stir 1 cup chicken broth into the rice mixture; cook, stirring frequently, until the broth is absorbed, 5 to 7 minutes. Continue with remaining broth, 1 cup at a time.
5. Remove saucepan from heat to add pumpkin puree, Gruyere cheese, Parmesan cheese, nutmeg, and cayenne pepper into the rice mixture, stirring until the cheese is melted and the mixture is smooth.

Bacon and Pine Nuts Pumpkin Risotto

Ingredients:

1/3 cup pine nuts
3 tbsps. olive oil
1 small onion, minced
Salt and ground black pepper to taste
2 cloves garlic, minced
1 1/2 cups Arborio rice
1/2 cup dry white wine
6 cups hot chicken stock
1 cup mashed pumpkin
1/4 cup butter
1/4 tsp. ground nutmeg
1/2 cup Parmesan cheese
3 slices crisply cooked bacon, crumbled
3 tbsps. chopped fresh chives
3 tbsps. chopped fresh basil

Directions:

1. Cook and stir pine nuts in a skillet over medium heat until fragrant and toasted, 2 to 5 minutes.
2. Heat olive oil in a large pot over medium-high heat; cook and stir onion in hot oil until soft, 4 to 7 minutes.
3. Add garlic, salt, and pepper; cook and stir until garlic is fragrant, about 30 seconds.
4. Stir Arborio rice into onion mixture; cook and stir until rice is coated with oil and lightly toasted, 1 to 3 minutes.
5. Pour white wine into rice mixture and cook, stirring constantly, until wine is completely absorbed, 3 to 5 minutes.
6. Pour hot chicken stock into rice mixture 1 ladle-full at a time, stirring until liquid is completely absorbed before adding the next, 3 to 7 minutes per ladle-full.
7. Stir pumpkin, butter, and nutmeg into rice mixture until well-combined; remove from heat.
8. Add Parmesan cheese, bacon, chives, and basil; stir until cheese is melted.

Roast Pumpkin and Feta Risotto

Ingredients:

3 1/4 cups peeled, cubed pumpkin
1 tbsp. olive oil
4 cups vegetable broth
1/2 tsp. chopped fresh garlic
1 onion, diced
1 cup baby spinach leaves
6 oz. feta cheese, cubed
Salt and pepper
2 cups Arborio rice

Directions:

1. Preheat oven to 400 degrees F (200 degrees C).
2. Brush a baking dish with olive oil.
3. Place pumpkin in a steamer over 1 inch of boiling water, and cover.
4. Cook until tender but still firm. Transfer pumpkin to baking dish, and brush with oil.
5. Season with salt and pepper.
6. Bake in preheated oven until golden brown.
7. Meanwhile, heat olive oil in a saucepan.
8. Cook onion and garlic until tender.
9. Stir in rice, and cook for 1 to 2 minutes.
10. Slowly add vegetable broth 1/2 cup at a time, stirring frequently and allowing all the liquid to be absorbed before adding more broth.
11. Continue cooking until the rice is tender to the tooth, and then season with salt and pepper to taste.
12. When the pumpkin is almost done, place feta on a baking sheet, and bake in preheated oven until the cheese is hot, and is beginning to melt along the edges.
13. Mash 1/2 of the pumpkin, and stir into the risotto with the spinach. Ladle risotto into bowls, and top with remaining pumpkin cubes and heated feta.

Barley Risotto Primavera

Ingredients:

2 tbsps. olive oil
2/3 cup carrots, peeled and chopped
1/2 cup finely chopped onion
2 garlic cloves, minced
1/2 tsp. dried thyme
3 cups cooked quick-cooking barley
1/2 cup white wine
2 cups vegetable broth, divided
1 cup zucchini, chopped
3/4 cup red bell pepper, chopped
3/4 cup yellow bell pepper, chopped
1/4 tsp. salt
Freshly ground black pepper, to taste
1 1/2 cups frozen peas
3/4 cup grated Parmesan cheese

Directions:

1. Heat oil in a large nonstick skillet over medium-high heat.
2. Add carrot and onion, and cook 4?5 minutes until onion begins to brown.
3. Add garlic and thyme; cook 1 minute or until fragrant.
4. Reduce heat to medium; stir in barley and white wine (if using) or 1/2 cup broth; cook 1 minute or until liquid is absorbed.
5. Add zucchini, bell peppers, and 3/4 cup broth; cook 4?5 minutes, stirring occasionally, until liquid is absorbed.
6. Add remaining 3/4 cup broth; cook until vegetables are tender and most of liquid has been absorbed.
7. Add 1/4 tsp. salt and freshly ground black pepper.
8. Stir in peas; remove from heat. Let stand 1?2 minutes or until peas are thawed but still bright green.
9. Stir in Parmesan cheese just before serving.

Herb Barley Risotto with Peas and Arugula

Ingredients:

1 tbsp. olive oil
1 shallot, finely chopped
1 clove garlic, minced
Salt and freshly ground black pepper
1/4 cup dry white wine
1 1/4 cups pearl barley
2 sprigs fresh thyme
1/3 cup finely grated pecorino
1 cup frozen peas
4 cups baby arugula, roughly chopped
2/3 cup chopped mixed herbs, such as parsley, basil and chives
2 tsps. fresh lemon juice

Directions:

1. In a pan, warm oil over medium heat.
2. Add shallot and garlic; cook, stirring occasionally, until tender, about 5 minutes.
3. Season with 1/4 tsp. each salt and pepper.
4. Add wine; cook until liquid has almost evaporated, 2 to 3 minutes.
5. Stir in barley and thyme; cook, stirring, for 1 minute.
6. Add 4 cups water and bring to a boil.
7. Cover, reduce heat to medium-low and simmer until barley is tender but still chewy, about 35 minutes.
8. Remove and discard thyme sprigs.
9. Add 1/4 tsp. salt, cheese and peas and stir until cheese is incorporated.
10. Stir in arugula, herbs and lemon juice. Divide among 4 bowls and drizzle with additional olive oil, if desired. Serve immediately.

Shrimp and Scallop Risotto

Shellfish Ingredients:

3 tbsps. olive oil
3 cloves garlic, peeled
1/2 pound shelled sea scallops
1/2 pound uncooked shrimp, peeled and deveined
Salt and ground black pepper to taste
1 pinch red pepper flakes
1/2 cup dry white wine
1/2 lemon, juiced
1 bunch fresh parsley, finely chopped

Risotto Ingredients:

1 quart fish stock, or more as needed
2 tbsps. butter
1 tbsp. olive oil
1 shallot, finely chopped
1 (12 oz.) package Arborio rice
1/2 cup dry white wine
1 tbsp. extra-virgin olive oil

Directions:

1. Heat 3 tbsps. olive oil in a skillet over a medium heat.
2. Add garlic; cook and stir until starting to sizzle, about 2 minutes.
3. Stir in scallops and cook for 1 minute.
4. Add shrimp and season with salt, pepper, and red pepper flakes.
5. Cook over high heat until shrimp are pink, 3 to 5 minutes.
6. Pour 1/2 cup white wine into the skillet and let the alcohol evaporate. Scrape the bottom of the skillet to deglaze; cook until the liquid is reduced, 2 to 3 minutes.
7. Remove from heat, add lemon juice, and sprinkle with 1/2 of the parsley. Discard garlic.
8. Cover the skillet to keep shellfish warm.
9. Pour fish stock into a saucepan over medium heat and bring to a simmer.
10. Melt butter in a skillet over low heat.
11. Add 1 tbsp. olive oil and shallot.
12. Cook until shallot is soft and translucent, but not brown, 3 to 5 minutes. Increase heat and add rice; cook until rice has absorbed the oil and butter and has a nutty aroma, stirring often, 1 to 2 minutes.
13. Make sure not to burn the shallot and reduce heat if skillet gets too hot.
14. Pour 1/2 cup white wine into the skillet and stir until alcohol has evaporated.
15. Add 1 ladleful of fish stock, stir, and cook until rice has absorbed the stock.

16. Add another ladleful and repeat the process until the rice is tender, 15 to 18 minutes in total.
17. Add shellfish with their juices to the risotto pan 3 minutes before the end of cooking.
18. Stir and finish cooking all together, adding stock if needed.
19. Remove from heat.
20. Stir in remaining parsley and 1 tbsp. extra-virgin olive oil. Let risotto stand for 2 minutes before serving.

Risotto with Truffle and Parmesan

Ingredients:

1 quart chicken broth
1 tbsp. butter
1 tbsp. olive oil
1/2 onion, minced
1 1/4 cups Arborio rice
1/2 cup white wine
2 tbsps. butter
2 tbsps. white truffle oil
1/3 cup grated Parmesan cheese
1 tsp. milk, or as needed
Salt and ground black pepper to taste
2 tbsps. chopped fresh parsley, or to taste

Directions:

1. Heat chicken broth in a stockpot over medium-low heat until warmed.
2. Heat 1 tbsp. butter and olive oil in a large, heavy-bottomed pan; cook and stir onion in the melted butter-oil mixture until translucent, about 2 minutes.
3. Add rice to onion mixture and stir to coat; cook and stir rice mixture until fragrant, about 1 minute.
4. Pour wine into rice mixture; cook and stir until liquid is absorbed, about 5 minutes.
5. Add 1 ladle of hot chicken broth to rice mixture, stirring constantly, until broth is absorbed. Continue adding 1 ladle of broth at a time until rice is tender but firm to the bite, 20 to 30 minutes.
6. Mix 2 tbsps. butter, truffle oil, Parmesan cheese, and milk into risotto until fully incorporated; season with salt, pepper, and parsley.

Green Risotto with Fava Beans

Ingredients:

1/2 pound fresh, unshelled fava beans
4 cups chicken broth
3 tbsps. butter, divided
1 small onion, finely chopped
1 cup Arborio rice
1/4 cup white wine
1/4 cup grated Reggiano Parmesan cheese
Salt to taste

Directions:

1. Bring a large pot of salted water to a boil.
2. Meanwhile, shell the favas and discard the pods.
3. Boil the favas for 4 minutes, strain and then immediately plunge into ice water. Let cool for 2 minutes then pierce the favas and squeeze them out of their skins. Separate 3/4 of the favas and puree in a food processor.
4. In a separate large saucepan bring the broth to a simmer, and keep it hot.
5. Meanwhile, in another large saucepan over medium heat, melt 1.5 tbsps. of the butter and add the onions.
6. Reduce the heat to low and cook for about 5 minutes; do not brown the onions.
7. Add the rice and cook, while stirring, for 2 minutes.
8. Add the wine, increase the heat to medium, and stir constantly.
9. When the wine has been absorbed, add a little of the hot stock.
10. Once the stock is absorbed, add a little more; repeat this process, stirring constantly, until the rice is cooked through.
11. To the cooked rice add the pureed favas, the remaining 1.5 tbsps. of butter, the rest of the favas and the cheese.
12. Cook over medium heat, stirring, until the butter and cheese melt and the puree is incorporated evenly.
13. Season with salt.

Farro Risotto

Ingredients:

1/2 cup dried porcini
1/2 cup recently boiled water
1/4 cup olive oil
1 leek, halved lengthwise and thinly sliced
2 3/4 cups pearled farro (perlato)
1/4 cup Marsala
5 cups broth, vegetable, chicken, or porcini
8 oz. crimini mushrooms sliced
1/2 tsp. dried thyme
1 clove garlic, peeled
1/4 cup ricotta
1/4 cup grated Parmesan
3 tbsps. chopped fresh parsley, to serve

Directions:

1. Cover the dried porcini with 1/2 cup of recently boiled water, then fill the kettle and put it on the heat again if you are making up the broth with concentrate, cube, or powder.
2. In a wide, heavy saucepan (that comes with a lid) add 2 tbsps. of the oil and the fine jade tangle of leek, and cook, stirring frequently, for about 5 minutes or until the leeks are softened.
3. Drain the porcini, reserving the soaking liquid, then chop them and add them to the pan.
4. Stir well, then add the farro and turn it gently but thoroughly in the pan. Tip in the Marsala and porcini-soaking water and let it bubble up.
5. Make up the broth as wished and add this to the farro pan, stir, bring to a boil, and then clamp on a lid, turn down the heat, and let it cook at a simmer for 30 minutes, until the farro is cooked and all the liquid absorbed.
6. While the farro is cooking, warm the remaining 2 tbsps. oil in a medium-sized frying pan and cook the sliced crimini mushrooms for about 5 minutes or until they begin to soften (they will first seem alarmingly dry) at which point add the thyme, grate in (or mince and add) the garlic, and cook for a further 5 minutes or until the mushrooms are juicy and soft.
7. Remove from the heat if there is still time on the clock for the farro. Once the farro is cooked, take it off the heat, too, and add the cooked mushrooms.
8. Stir in the ricotta and Parmesan (they will melt in the heat of the farro) until the farro is creamy, then sprinkle with parsley and serve.

Italian Wedding Risotto Soup

Ingredients:

6 oz. bulk sweet Italian sausage
1 tbsp. canola oil
1/2 cup minced shallots
1 tbsp. minced garlic
1/4 tsp. crushed red pepper
4 cups unsalted chicken stock
1 1/2 cups prepared risotto
1 cup chopped escarole
1/4 tsp. kosher salt
1/4 shaved Parmesan cheese

Directions:

1. Divide and shape sausage into 26 balls (about 1 tsp. each).
2. Heat a large Dutch oven over medium heat.
3. Add oil; swirl.
4. Add minced shallots, minced garlic, and crushed red pepper; sauté 5 minutes.
5. Add chicken stock; bring to a boil.
6. Add sausage and prepared risotto reserved from Sweet Onion Risotto with Sautéed Kale; reduce heat, and simmer 5 minutes.
7. Stir in escarole and salt; cook 2 minutes. Divide among 4 bowls; top with shaved Parmesan cheese.

Prawn and Pine Nut Risotto

Ingredients:

2 tbsps. olive oil
1 onion, finely chopped
2 cups Arborio rice
1/2 cup white wine
1 quart chicken broth, warmed
1/4 cup chile-garlic flavored butter
12 oz. medium shrimp, peeled and deveined, tails left on
1 carrot, cut into thin strips
1/3 cup pine nuts
1/4 cup sliced black olives
1 large red chile pepper, minced
Ground black pepper to taste

Directions:

1. Heat olive oil in a large saucepan over medium heat.
2. Stir in the onion and cook until softened and translucent, about 3 minutes.
3. Stir in Arborio rice until well coated in oil; continue cooking until both the onion and rice begin to turn golden-brown, about 8 minutes.
4. Pour in the white wine and stir until evaporated.
5. Pour in 1/3 of the hot chicken broth; stir constantly as the risotto simmers and slowly absorbs the broth, about 8 minutes.
6. Add half of the remaining broth, and continue stirring until absorbed, about another 8 minutes.
7. Stir in chile-garlic butter, shrimp, carrot, pine nuts, black olives, and red chile pepper until the butter has melted.
8. Stir in the remaining chicken broth, and again stir constantly until absorbed, about 8 minutes.
9. Season to taste with black pepper.
10. At this point, taste the rice; it should be slightly firm and totally delicious. If it is still a little crunchy, stir in some hot water and continue cooking until it reaches the desired tenderness.

Wild Risotto

Ingredients:

5 cups water
1/4 cup uncooked wild rice
2 tsps. olive oil
6 green onions, chopped
2 cloves garlic, minced
1 1/2 cups uncooked Arborio rice
1/2 cup white wine
1 tsp. chopped fresh tarragon
2 roma plum tomatoes, chopped
2/3 cup coconut milk
1 cup frozen green peas, thawed

Directions:

1. In a saucepan, bring 1 cup water to a boil.
2. Add the wild rice, cover the pan, and reduce the heat. Simmer for 25 minutes; drain well.
3. Bring 4 cups water to simmer in a large saucepan. Keep the water simmering while you begin step number 3.
4. Heat the olive oil in a large frying pan. Saute the scallions and garlic over medium-high heat for 1 minute.
5. Add the Arborio rice; stir it for 2 minutes.
6. Pour the wine, the wild rice, and the tarragon into the frying pan.
7. Cook, stirring frequently, for 2 minutes.
8. Pour 1/2 cup of the heated water into the frying pan.
9. Stir frequently until the liquid is absorbed, then add 1/2 cup more water.
10. Continue adding the water in this manner, waiting between additions until the liquid is absorbed and stirring frequently.
11. After about 18 to 20 minutes most of the liquid should be absorbed, and the rice should be tender but still slightly chewy.
12. When all of the water is absorbed, add the tomatoes, coconut milk, and peas.
13. Stir in the mixture, and simmer it, stirring often, until most of the liquid is absorbed. Serve at once.

Barley Risotto with Eggplant and Tomatoes

Ingredients:

6 cups diced eggplant
1 pint cherry tomatoes
3 tbsps. olive oil, divided
1/2 tsp. black pepper, divided
5 cups chicken broth
2 cups water
1 1/2 cups finely chopped onion
1 cup uncooked pearl barley
2 tsps. minced garlic
1/2 cup dry white wine

Directions:

1. Preheat oven to 400 degrees F.
2. Combine eggplant, tomatoes, 2 tbsps. oil, and 1/4 tsp. pepper in a bowl; toss to coat.
3. Arrange mixture in a single layer on a jelly-roll pan.
4. Bake at 400° for 20 minutes or until tomatoes begin to collapse and eggplant is tender.
5. Combine broth and 2 cups water in a medium saucepan; bring to a simmer (do not boil). Keep warm over low heat.
6. Heat remaining 1 tbsp. oil in a large nonstick skillet over medium-high heat.
7. Add onion to pan; sauté 4 minutes or until onion begins to brown.
8. Stir in barley and garlic; cook 1 minute.
9. Add wine; cook 1 minute or until liquid almost evaporates, stirring constantly.
10. Add 1 cup broth mixture to pan; bring to a boil, stirring frequently.
11. Cook 5 minutes or until liquid is nearly absorbed, stirring constantly.
12. Add remaining broth mixture, 1 cup at a time, stirring constantly until each portion of broth mixture is absorbed before adding the next (about 40 minutes total).
13. Gently stir in eggplant mixture, remaining 1/4 tsp. pepper, and salt.
14. Top with cheese, basil, and nuts.

Gorgonzola and Wild Mushroom Risotto

Ingredients:

2 oz. dried chanterelle mushrooms
1 1/2 tsps. butter
1 tsp. truffle oil
1 chopped onion
2 shallots, minced
1 clove garlic, minced
3 oz. sliced fresh button mushrooms
1 (12 oz.) package Arborio rice
1/2 cup dry white wine
1 quart hot chicken stock
2 tbsps. heavy cream
2 tbsps. crumbled Gorgonzola cheese
Ground black pepper to taste

Directions:

1. Cover chanterelle mushrooms with hot water, cover, and set aside to soften for 30 minutes. Once soft, remove the mushrooms from the water and chop; discard water.
2. Melt butter along with truffle oil in a large saucepan over medium-high heat.
3. Add the onion, shallot, and garlic; cook and stir two minutes until the onion begins to soften.
4. Add the fresh mushrooms, and continue cooking until the mushroom softens and begins to release its liquid.
5. Stir in the chopped chanterelle mushrooms, and cook 3 minutes more.
6. Add Arborio rice; cook and stir for a few minutes until the rice is well coated with the onion mixture and looks glossy.
7. Stir in the white wine, and cook until nearly evaporated.
8. Reduce heat to medium, and add 1/3 of the hot chicken stock.
9. Cook and stir until the chicken stock has been mostly absorbed, about 5 minutes.
10. The risotto should be simmering gently while you stir in the chicken stock.
11. Add half of the remaining stock, and stir for 5 minutes more.
12. Finally add the remaining stock, and continue cooking until the risotto is creamy and the rice is tender, about 5 minutes more.
13. The rice should not be completely soft, but still have a little firmness when you bite into it. You can add a little water if needed to cook the rice to this state.
14. Remove the risotto from the heat, and stir in the heavy cream and Gorgonzola cheese.

15. Season to taste with salt and pepper, and serve.

Creamy Edamame Risotto

Ingredients:

1 tbsp. sesame oil
1 1/2 cups frozen shelled edamame
1 tbsp. soy sauce
3/4 tsp. ground ginger
2 tbsps. olive oil
1 cup Arborio rice
1/2 tsp. garlic powder
1/2 cup dry white wine
4 cups hot water
1/4 cup crumbled goat cheese
2 tbsps. grated Parmesan cheese
1 1/2 tsps. dried basil
1/4 tsp. ground ginger
Salt and pepper to taste

Directions:

1. Heat the sesame oil in a skillet over medium heat.
2. Stir in the edamame, soy sauce, and 3/4 tsps. of ground ginger.
3. Cook and stir until the edamame is hot and the liquid has evaporated, about 5 minutes. Set aside.
4. Meanwhile, heat the olive oil in a large, heavy-bottomed saucepan over medium-high heat.
5. Pour in the rice, and stir until the rice is coated in oil and has started to toast, 2 to 3 minutes.
6. Reduce the heat to medium and stir in the garlic powder and white wine. Let the wine simmer until it has mostly evaporated, then stir in one-third of the hot water; continue stirring until the rice has absorbed the liquid and turned creamy.
7. Repeat this process twice more, stirring constantly.
8. Stirring in the water should take 15 to 20 minutes in all. When finished, the rice should be tender, yet slightly firm.
9. Stir in the edamame, goat cheese, Parmesan cheese, basil, and 1/4 tsp. of ground ginger until the cheeses have melted.
10. Season to taste with salt and pepper before serving.

Sweet Pea Risotto

Ingredients:

1 tbsp. unsalted butter
1 tbsp. olive oil
1/2 yellow onion, chopped
2 cups Arborio rice
1 cup dry white wine (such as Sauvignon Blanc)
4 cups chicken broth
1 cup freshly grated Parmesan
1 tsp. kosher salt
1/4 tsp. freshly ground black pepper
2 1/2 cups frozen peas, thawed
Fresh mint sprigs

Directions:

1. Heat the butter and oil together in a large skillet or saucepan over medium heat.
2. Add the onion and sauté until translucent, 3 to 4 minutes.
3. Add the rice and stir to coat in the oil and butter.
4. Pour in the wine, then stir until all the liquid is absorbed.
5. Reduce heat to low.
6. Add 1 cup of the broth and cook until absorbed, stirring occasionally.
7. Add the remaining broth, 1/2 cup at a time, waiting until each portion of broth is absorbed before adding the next. Continue this process until the rice is cooked al dente, about 40 minutes.
8. Stir in the Parmesan, salt, and pepper. Puree 2 cups of the peas in a blender or food processor. Just before serving, stir in the pea puree until fully incorporated, then fold in the remaining whole peas. Garnish with mint sprigs, if desired. Serve immediately.

Creamy Quinoa Risotto

Ingredients:

1 cup quinoa
5 cups chicken broth, or as needed
3 tbsps. unsalted butter
1 small yellow onion, chopped
2 cloves garlic, minced
1/2 cup dry white wine
1/2 cup freshly grated Parmesan cheese
1 tbsp. heavy whipping cream
1/4 tsp. dried marjoram
1/4 tsp. dried thyme
Salt and pepper to taste

Directions:

1. Rinse quinoa twice and drain well.
2. Pour chicken broth into a saucepan; bring to a boil.
3. Melt butter in a separate saucepan over medium-high heat; saute onion and garlic until onion is soft, about 5 minutes.
4. Stir quinoa into onion mixture; cook, stirring frequently, until quinoa is toasted and coated in oil, about 3 minutes.
5. Slowly pour wine over quinoa mixture; cook and stir until wine is absorbed, about 5 minutes. Ladle 1/2 cup chicken broth over quinoa mixture; cook, stirring frequently, until absorbed, 3 to 5 minutes. Continue ladling broth, 1/2 cup at a time, over quinoa mixture; cook, stirring frequently, until quinoa is tender and has burst, about 20 minutes. You may not use all the chicken broth.
6. Mix Parmesan cheese and cream into quinoa mixture; season with marjoram, thyme, salt, and pepper.
7. Add a splash of chicken broth to make quinoa more creamy, if desired.

Lobster Risotto

Ingredients:

4 cups chicken broth
3 (5-oz.) American lobster tails
3 tbsps. butter, divided
1 cup uncooked Arborio rice
3/4 cup frozen green peas, thawed

Directions:

1. Bring broth and 1 1/2 cups water to a boil in a saucepan.
2. Add lobster; cover and cook for 4 minutes.
3. Remove lobster from pan; cool for 5 minutes.
4. Remove meat from cooked lobster tails, reserving shells. Chop meat.
5. Place shells in a large zip-top plastic bag. Coarsely crush shells using a meat mallet or heavy skillet. Return crushed shells to the broth mixture.
6. Reduce heat to medium-low.
7. Cover and cook for 20 minutes. Strain shell mixture through a sieve over a bowl, reserving broth; discard solids. Return broth mixture to saucepan; keep warm over low heat. Heat 1 tbsp. butter in a medium saucepan over medium-high heat.
8. Add rice to pan; cook 2 minutes, stirring constantly.
9. Stir in 1 cup broth mixture, and cook for 5 minutes or until liquid is nearly absorbed, stirring constantly. Reserve 2 tbsps. broth mixture.
10. Add the remaining broth mixture, 1/2 cup at a time, stirring constantly until each portion is absorbed before adding the next (about 22 minutes total).
11. Remove from heat, and stir in lobster, the reserved 2 tbsps. broth mixture, 2 tbsps. butter, and green peas.

Shrimp and Fennel Risotto

Ingredients:

1 (32 oz.) container chicken broth
1 tbsp. butter
1 1/2 cups finely chopped fennel bulb
1/4 cup minced shallots
2 garlic cloves, minced
1 cup uncooked Arborio rice
2/3 cup dry white wine
1 1/2 pounds peeled and deveined shrimp
1 1/2 tbsps. minced fennel fronds
1 tsp. grated lemon rind
1/2 tsp. freshly ground black pepper
1/3 cup shredded fresh Parmesan cheese, divided

Directions:

1. Bring broth to a simmer in a medium saucepan (do not boil). Keep warm over low heat.
2. Melt butter in a large saucepan over medium-high heat.
3. Add fennel bulb, shallots, and garlic, and sauté 4 minutes or until tender.
4. Add rice, and cook 2 minutes, stirring constantly.
5. Add wine, and cook until liquid is nearly absorbed, stirring constantly.
6. Add warm broth, 1/2 cup at a time, stirring constantly; cook until each portion of broth is absorbed before adding the next (about 30 minutes total).
7. Stir in shrimp, fennel fronds, lemon rind, and pepper; cook 8 minutes or until shrimp are done, stirring occasionally.
8. Stir in 1/4 cup Parmesan cheese. Spoon risotto into bowls; sprinkle with remaining Parmesan cheese.

Chanterelle Mushroom Risotto

Ingredients:

4 oz. bacon, diced
2 tbsps. olive oil
1 onion (8 oz.) peeled, halved lengthwise, and thinly sliced
1 tbsp. minced garlic
1/4 tsp. salt
1/4 tsp. pepper
1 bunch (10 to 12 oz.) red chard
2 cups arborio (short-grain white) rice
1 cup dry white wine
6 cups chicken broth
1/4 cup shredded parmesan cheese
2 tbsps. butter
Roasted chanterelle mushrooms

Directions:

1. In a 12-inch frying pan with 2-inch-tall sides or a 5-quart pan over medium-high heat, stir bacon until browned and crisp, about 5 minutes. Transfer to paper towels to drain. Discard all but about 1/2 tbsp. bacon fat from pan.
2. Add 2 tbsps. olive oil to pan over medium-high heat. When hot, add onion, garlic, salt, and pepper.
3. Reduce heat to medium and stir frequently until onion is very soft and browned, 20 to 25 minutes (if onion starts to scorch, reduce heat further and stir in 2 tbsps. water).
4. Meanwhile, rinse chard. Trim and discard stem ends. Thinly slice stems crosswise and coarsely chop leaves.
5. In a 5- to 6-quart pan over high heat, bring about 3 quarts water to a boil.
6. Add chard and cook, stirring occasionally, until stems are tender-crisp to bite, 3 to 4 minutes.
7. Drain, place in a large bowl of ice water until cool, and drain again.
8. Add rice to onions and stir until opaque, about 3 minutes.
9. Add wine and stir over medium heat until absorbed, 1 to 2 minutes.
10. Add 6 cups broth, a cup at a time, stirring after each addition until almost absorbed, 20 to 25 minutes total (rice should be tender to bite).
11. Stir in cheese, butter, bacon, chard, and roasted mushrooms. If risotto is thicker than desired, stir in a little more broth. Spoon risotto into wide, shallow bowls.

Creamy Corn Risotto

Ingredients:

1 large red bell pepper
4 cups corn kernels
2 tbsps. butter, divided
2 1/2 cups unsalted chicken stock
1/2 cup chopped onion
2 tsps. minced garlic
1 cup uncooked Arborio rice
1 tsp. salt
1 tsp. freshly ground black pepper
1/4 cup dry white wine
1/2 cup sliced green onions

Directions:

1. Preheat broiler to high.
2. Cut bell pepper in half lengthwise; discard seeds and membranes.
3. Place pepper halves, skin sides up, on a foil-lined baking sheet; flatten with hand. Broil 8 minutes or until blackened.
4. Wrap peppers in foil; let stand 5 minutes.
5. Peel and chop.
6. Combine corn, milk, and 1 tbsp. butter in a saucepan.
7. Bring to a simmer; cook 10 minutes.
8. Stir in stock; keep warm over low heat.
9. Melt remaining 1 tbsp. butter in a large saucepan over medium-high heat; swirl to coat.
10. Add onion and garlic to pan; sauté 3 minutes.
11. Stir in rice, salt, and black pepper; sauté 2 minutes, stirring constantly.
12. Stir in wine; cook 30 seconds or until liquid almost evaporates, scraping pan to loosen browned bits.
13. Reduce heat to medium.
14. Stir in 1 1/2 cups corn mixture; cook 3 minutes or until liquid is nearly absorbed, stirring constantly. Reserve 1/2 cup corn mixture.
15. Add remaining corn mixture, 1 cup at a time, stirring frequently until each portion of corn mixture is absorbed before adding the next (about 20 minutes total).
16. Remove pan from heat; stir in 1/2 cup corn mixture, bell pepper, and green onions.

Cauliflower Risotto Cakes

Ingredients:

1 pound cauliflower florets
1 1/2 cups prepared risotto reserved
2/3 cup panko breadcrumbs
1/4 cup chopped flat-leaf parsley
1/2 tsp. kosher salt
1/2 tsp. black pepper
2 oz. shredded fontina cheese
1 large egg
2 tbsps. olive oil, divided
2 tbsps. canola mayonnaise
1 tbsp. lemon juice
2 tsps. minced fresh chives
1 garlic clove, minced

Directions:

1. Preheat oven to 400 degrees F. Pulse cauliflower florets in a food processor until finely chopped.
2. Spread on a baking sheet; bake at 400° for 40 minutes, stirring occasionally.
3. Combine cauliflower, prepared risotto reserved from Sweet Onion Risotto with Sautéed Kale, panko, parsley, salt, pepper, fontina cheese, and egg; shape into 8 (3-inch) patties. Heat 1 tbsp. olive oil in a large nonstick skillet over medium heat.
4. Add 4 patties to pan; cook 3 minutes on each side.
5. Remove from pan.
6. Repeat procedure with 1 tbsp. olive oil and remaining 4 patties.
7. Combine mayonnaise, lemon juice, chives, and minced garlic. Serve with patties.

Chicken Risotto

Ingredients:

3 tbsps. butter
1 cup minced sweet onion
2 garlic cloves, pressed
1 cup Arborio rice
1/4 cup dry white wine
4 cups chicken broth
1 (14-oz.) can quartered artichoke hearts, drained
3 cups chopped cooked chicken
2 cups zucchini, chopped
1/2 tsp. freshly ground pepper
1/2 cup grated Parmesan cheese
1/4 cup chopped fresh parsley
1 tsp. lemon zest

Directions:

1. Preheat oven to 425 degrees F.
2. Melt butter in a Dutch oven over medium-high heat; add onion and garlic, and sauté 5 minutes.
3. Add rice, and cook 2 minutes or until golden brown.
4. Add wine, and cook 2 to 3 minutes or until wine is absorbed.
5. Add chicken broth.
6. Bring to a boil, cover, and transfer to oven.
7. Bake 20 minutes.
8. Remove rice from oven, and stir in artichokes and next 3 ingredients.
9. Cover and bake 10 minutes.
10. Remove from oven, and let stand 5 minutes.
11. Stir in cheese and remaining ingredients. Serve immediately.

Risotto with Pesto

Ingredients:

2 tbsps. unsalted butter
1 small yellow onion, finely chopped
2 cups Arborio rice
1 cup dry white wine
4 cups chicken broth
1 cup grated Parmesan
1/2 tsp. kosher salt
1/4 tsp. black pepper
1/3 cup store-bought pesto

Directions:

1. Melt the butter in a large saucepan over medium heat.
2. Add the onion and cook for 3 minutes.
3. Add the rice and cook, stirring constantly, for 2 minutes.
4. Reduce heat to medium-low.
5. Add the wine and cook, stirring frequently, until the liquid is absorbed.
6. Add the broth, 1/2 cup at a time, stirring occasionally and waiting until it's absorbed before adding more.
7. It should take about 30 minutes for all the broth to be absorbed.
8. Remove from heat and stir in the Parmesan, salt, and pepper, then stir in the pesto. Spoon into individual bowls.

Risotto Milanese

Ingredients:

5 cups unsalted chicken stock
1 1/2 tbsps. extra-virgin olive oil
1 1/4 cups diced onion
1 1/2 cups Arborio rice
5/8 tsp. kosher salt
1/4 tsp. saffron threads, crushed
1/2 cup dry white wine
1 tbsp. butter
1/2 tsp. freshly ground black pepper
1/3 cup Parmigiano-Reggiano cheese, grated
2 tbsps. chopped fresh flat-leaf parsley

Directions:

1. Bring stock to a simmer in a saucepan (do not boil). Keep warm over low heat.
2. Heat a Dutch oven over medium heat.
3. Add oil to pan; swirl to coat.
4. Add onion; cook 5 minutes, stirring occasionally.
5. Add rice, salt, and saffron; cook 1 minute, stirring frequently.
6. Add wine; cook 2 minutes or until liquid is absorbed, stirring frequently.
7. Stir in 1 1/2 cups stock; cook 4 minutes or until liquid is nearly absorbed, stirring constantly.
8. Add remaining stock, 3/4 cup at a time, stirring nearly constantly until each portion is absorbed before adding the next (about 22 minutes total); reserve 1/3 cup stock at last addition.
9. Remove pan from heat.
10. Stir in reserved 1/3 cup stock, butter, pepper, and cheese. Top with parsley.

Risotto Alle Vongole (Risotto with Clams)

Ingredients:

3 dozen littleneck clams (about 2 1/2 pounds)
8 1/2 cups water, divided
3 tbsps. olive oil, divided
2 tbsps. chopped fresh flat-leaf parsley
2 tsps. minced garlic
1 1/2 cups Arborio rice
1/4 tsp. salt
1/4 tsp. freshly ground black pepper
Chopped fresh parsley

Directions:

1. Put the clams and 1/2 cup water in a large skillet over medium-high heat; cover and cook for 4 minutes or until the shells open.
2. Remove the clams from the pan, reserving the cooking liquid. Cool clams.
3. Remove the meat from the shells, and set aside.
4. Bring 8 cups water to a simmer in a large saucepan (do not boil). Keep warm over low heat.
5. Put 2 tbsps. olive oil, parsley, and garlic in a large saucepan; cook over medium-high heat until garlic sizzles.
6. Add the rice, and stir until coated; cook for 5 minutes, stirring constantly.
7. Stir in reserved clam liquid; cook until the liquid is absorbed, stirring constantly.
8. Add water, 1 cup at a time, stirring constantly until each portion of water is absorbed before adding the next. Continue until rice is tender.
9. Season with salt and pepper.
10. Add clams; cook 3 minutes or until thoroughly heated.
11. Stir in 1 tbsp. olive oil, and sprinkle with parsley, if desired. Serve immediately.
12. Note: To substitute canned clams for the fresh, use 3 (6-oz.) cans clams, undrained, and use 7 cups water.

Caramelized Carrot Risotto

Ingredients:

2 tbsps. vegetable oil, divided
3 tbsps. unsalted butter, divided
3 cups (6 medium) carrots, finely chopped
1/2 tsp. salt
1 tsp. sugar
5 cups reduced-sodium chicken broth
1/3 cup minced onion
1 1/2 cups Arborio rice
1/2 cup dry white wine
1/4 cup mascarpone cheese
1/4 cup freshly shredded parmesan cheese, plus 1/2 cups for garnish
1 tbsp. finely chopped flat-leaf parsley, plus 1 tbsp. for garnish
1 tsp. roughly chopped fresh thyme
1/8 tsp. white pepper

Directions:

1. Heat 1 tbsp. oil and 1 tbsp. butter over medium heat in a medium heavy-bottomed pot.
2. Add carrots and stir with a wooden spoon until well coated.
3. Add 1/2 cup water, 1/2 tsp. salt, and the sugar; cover and cook 5 minutes, or until tender.
4. Uncover and cook, stirring occasionally, until water evaporates and carrots are just starting to brown, a few minutes more. Reserve half of the carrots.
5. In a blender, purée other half with 3/4 cup hot water.
6. Bring chicken broth to a simmer and keep at a simmer, covered, over low heat.
7. Heat remaining oil and butter over medium heat in same (unwashed) pot used for carrots.
8. Add onion and cook until translucent, about 3 minutes.
9. Add rice, stirring with a wooden spoon to coat rice with oil, 1 minute.
10. Add wine and cook, stirring, until wine evaporates.
11. Add carrot purée and cook, stirring, until mixture no longer looks soupy.
12. Add 1/2 cup hot broth, stirring often, until rice absorbs most of the liquid.
13. Repeat process, adding 1/2 cup broth at a time and stirring often till each addition is absorbed before adding the next, until rice is al dente (about 20 minutes; at least 1 cup broth will remain).
14. Fold in reserved carrots (save 2 tbsp. for garnish), mascarpone, 1/4 cup parmesan, 1 tbsp. parsley, and the thyme.
15. Add up to 1 cup broth (1/4 cup at a time) to loosen the risotto.
16. Season with salt and white pepper to taste.
17. Sprinkle each bowl of risotto with some of remaining 1/2 cup parmesan, remaining 1 tbsp. parsley, and reserved carrots. Serve immediately.

Creamy Maple Bacon Pumpkin Risotto

Ingredients:

4 thick slices bacon, diced
2 cups apple cider or juice (not spiced)
4 cups chicken or vegetable stock
1 1/2 cup leeks white and green part only, diced
4 garlic cloves, minced
2 cups Arborio rice
1 cup dry white wine
1/4 tsp. freshly grated nutmeg
1 tsp. sea salt
1/2 tsp. ground black pepper
1 1/2 cup pumpkin puree (fresh or canned, not pumpkin pie filling)
2 tbsps. pure maple syrup
Italian flat leaf parsley

Directions:

1. In a medium saucepan combine the chicken or vegetable stock and apple cider and set over very low heat.
2. In a stock pot or deep sided sauté pan cook the bacon over medium heat until crispy, about 10 minutes, being careful not to burn.
3. Remove with a slotted spoon to paper towels to drain.
4. Drain off all but 2 tbsp of the bacon fat and add the leeks and sauté until caramelized, about 8 minutes.
5. Add in the garlic and nutmeg and sauté until fragrant, another 30 seconds.
6. Add in the rice and the wine and stir well until the wine is cooked down. Turn the heat under the chicken stock to medium.
7. Add in ½ cup of chicken stock mixture to the rice mixture and stir until absorbed.
8. Repeat with ½ a cup at a time until the rice is al-dente, stirring well after each addition. You may not end up using all the chicken stock mixture.
9. Mix in the pumpkin puree and maple syrup and stir. Taste and season with salt and pepper. If the rice is chewier than desired add more chicken stock in and stir.
10. Stir in the bacon and serve immediately. Top with chopped Italian parsley and a little grated parmesan cheese.

Bacon, Cheddar & Beer Risotto

Ingredients:

1 tbsp. light butter
1/2 small onion, chopped
2 garlic cloves, minced
2 cups uncooked Arborio rice
12 oz. bottle of beer
6 cups chicken broth
1 1/2 oz. Parmesan cheese, freshly grated
3/4 cup sharp shredded cheddar cheese
2/3 cup shredded cheddar cheese
4 slices cooked extra lean turkey bacon
1/4 tsp. cayenne pepper

Directions:

1. Place the butter in a large sauté pan and bring it over medium-low heat until butter is just melted.
2. Add onions and cook 3-5 minutes until the onions are translucent.
3. Add the garlic and cook for another minute until garlic is fragrant.
4. Add the rice and stir to combine.
5. Cook an additional 2 minutes, stirring throughout.
6. Pour in the beer and turn the heat up to high until the beer begins to simmer.
7. Reduce heat back to medium-low and add ½ cup of the chicken broth.
8. Stir until the liquid dissolves and then add another ½ cup.
9. Repeat until all the broth has been added and the rice is creamy and al dente.
10. Remove the rice mixture from the heat and add the cheeses, bacon and cayenne pepper.
11. Stir until thoroughly combined and serve.

Red Wine Risotto

Ingredients:

32 oz. of chicken broth
20 oz. package of Sweet Italian Sausage
8 oz. baby bella mushrooms chopped small
1 cup arborio rice
1 cup red wine

Directions:

1. Heat the chicken broth over low heat. You could either use chicken broth by the can or box, or buy a small jar of broth base and add it to four cups of boiling water, turning the heat to a low simmer once it is combined. I prefer to use the base because it is much less expensive and I find myself using chicken broth so often.
2. Over medium high heat, remove the sausage from the casing and cook it in an oiled pan. (I like to just coat the inside of the pan in a spray of olive oil.) Season lightly with salt and pepper. Break it up as it cooks, stirring every few minutes until it is just cooked through, approximately 8 minutes.
3. Add the chopped mushrooms and cook until they are softened, approximately 3 minutes.
4. Turn the heat down to medium low.
5. Add the arborio rice, and stir. The rice will quickly soak up the cooking liquid from the sausage and the mushrooms.
6. Once there is minimal liquid left in the pan, add the wine, continuing to stir occasionally, approximately 6 minutes.
7. After the wine is absorbed, add the warm chicken broth one cup at a time until it is absorbed and the risotto is tender, approximately 15 minutes.

Caprese Risotto

Ingredients:

2 tbsps. olive oil, & then some for drizzling
2 cloves of garlic, minced
4 cups of chicken or vegetable broth
1 1/2 cups of arborio rice
1/2 cup white wine (optional)
1 tbsp. butter
2/3 cup shredded mozzarella cheese
Fresh basil leaves
Grape or cherry tomatoes

Directions:

1. Pour the chicken broth into a large saucepan. Over medium-low heat, start to slowly heat the broth to a low simmer.
2. Heat the 2 tbsp of olive oil over medium heat in a large dutch oven. Then add in the garlic and saute for a quick minute or two.
3. Add the cup of arborio rice to the garlic. Saute for another 1-2 minutes to slightly toast the rice.
4. Pour in your white wine now if you are choosing to add this.
5. Cook and stir the rice/wine mixture over medium heat until all the liquid is absorbed.
6. If you are skipping the wine in this dish, then just move on to the next step below.
7. Using a ladle, scoop in one ladle full of the chicken broth.
8. Cook and stir over medium-low heat until all the liquid is once again absorbed.
9. Continue doing this- ladling in the broth, stirring until absorbed until you have used all the chicken broth. This entire process should take between 30-35 minutes.
10. Once your risotto has absorbed all the liquid, remove from the heat and stir in the shredded mozzarella cheese and butter.
11. Season with salt and pepper to taste.
12. Top with fresh grape or cherry tomatoes and basil leaf chiffonades. You can choose to leave the tomatoes raw, or do as I did and give them a quick saute in a small frying pan with a little bit of olive oil. I only cooked them for about 2 minutes. You want them to remain whole and not get so hot that they burst open.
13. Finish each plate with a little drizzle of olive oil and enjoy!

Broccoli Cheddar Risotto

Ingredients:

4 cups chicken or vegetable stock
2 tbsps. olive oil
6 slices bacon, minced
1 medium onion, diced
1 cup Arborio rice
1 1/2 tbsps. lemon juice mixed with 2 1/2 tbsps. water
2 large cloves garlic, minced
2 cups broccoli florets, chopped small
1/8 tsp. black pepper
3 oz sharp cheddar, grated
2 tbsps. minced fresh parsley leaves, for garnish

Directions:

1. Bring chicken stock to a simmer in a medium saucepan over medium heat; turn heat down to low so it stays hot as you cook the risotto.
2. Heat the oil in a separate medium saucepan over medium heat; add the turkey bacon and cook until crispy, about 5 minutes.
3. Remove the turkey bacon with a slotted spoon and set aside for now. Add the onion to the oil you cooked the turkey bacon in and cook until soft but not brown, about 5 minutes, stirring occasionally.
4. Add the rice and cook until slightly browned and nutty smelling, about 3 to 4 minutes, stirring occasionally.
5. Add the lemon juice/water mixture and cook until evaporated, about 1 minute. Stir in the garlic, broccoli, and black pepper.
6. Turn heat down to medium-low.
7. Add 1/2 cup of the hot stock to the rice, stirring constantly until the liquid is almost completely absorbed, then adding more stock in the same manner.
8. Continue this way until the risotto is tender with just a slight bite to it, about 20 to 25 minutes.
9. You may need slightly more or less liquid to achieve this; if you run out of stock, you can just simmer some water.
10. Turn off heat and stir in the cheese and turkey bacon; add salt and pepper to taste. Sprinkle parsley on top (if using) and serve immediately.

Spinach Basil Pesto Risotto

Pesto Ingredients:

2 cloves garlic
2 cups packed basil leaves
1 cup spinach leaves
1/4 cup olive oil
3 tbsps. fresh lemon juice
kosher salt

Tomatoes Ingredients:

2 cups cherry tomatoes
2 tbsps. olive oil
Kosher salt

Risotto Ingredients:

4 tbsps. olive oil
1/2 yellow onion, diced small
1 1/2 cup arborio rice
1 cup dry white wine
5 cups vegetable or chicken stock
kosher salt
fresh basil, for garnish

Directions:

1. Preheat oven to 400 degrees F.
2. To make the pesto, combine garlic, basil, spinach, olive oil and lemon juice in the jar of a blender. Puree until smooth and then season with kosher salt. Set aside.
3. Place cherry tomatoes on a sheet pan prepared with a sheet of parchment paper.
4. Drizzle with the olive oil and sprinkle with kosher salt.
5. Place in the oven and roast for 15 minutes.
6. For the risotto, in a large pan over medium heat, add the olive oil and onion. Saute the onion, stirring often, about 5 minutes.
7. Add rice and stir to coat the rice with the onion and oil.
8. Cook, stirring often, for 2 minutes.
9. Meanwhile, bring stock to a simmer over low heat in a small pot near by the pan.
10. Add wine to rice and stir, scraping any bits from the bottom of the pan. As the wine cooks off, add a large ladle of stock and continue to cook and stir. As the stock cooks off, add another ladle of stock.
11. Continue this process of adding stock and cooking it off, stirring continuously.

12. When you are about 20 minutes in and have added most of the stock, add the spinach-basil pesto and the rest of the broth. Continue to cook another 2 minutes or until rice is tender and cooked through.
13. Season to taste with kosher salt.
14. Spoon into serving bowls and top with the roasted cherry tomatoes and a drizzle of olive oil. Garnish with fresh basil if desired.

Crispy mozzarella risotto cakes

Ingredients:

1 1/2 cups leftover cold risotto
6 1/2-in. cubes mozzarella
1/3 cup vegetable oil

Directions:

1. Scoop about 1/4 cup risotto into palm of hand. Flatten slightly and press 1 cube of cheese (or 1 tsp goat cheese) into centre. Shape risotto into a ball around cheese.
2. Roll ball in panko, then place on a baking sheet.
3. Repeat with remaining rice, cheese and panko.
4. Heat a large frying pan over medium high.
5. Pour enough oil to come to 1/2 in. up the side, about 1/3 cup. When oil is hot, carefully place risotto balls into the pan and flatten slightly. (Do not crowd pan.
6. Cook in 2 batches if necessary.) Fry until golden, 3 to 4 min per side.
7. Remove to a paper-towel-lined plate.

Seafood Risotto

Ingredients:

1 cooked whole lobster, claws and tail, diced
8 shrimp, cooked peeled and deveined, diced
6 large scallops, cooked and diced
1 1/2 quart of seafood stock
cup arborio rice
2 large shallots
3/4 cup of Prosecco or white wine
1 cup of canned or fresh diced tomatoes, drained of wet liquid
Parsley
Olive oil and butter

Directions:

1. Cook the shrimp and scallops on a foil lined sheet pan, drizzle seafood with some garlic infused olive oil and a small handful of chopped parsley, roast at 425 degrees until pink and translucent, maybe 10 minutes, let it rest.
2. Break down your whole lobster tail, removing the shell from the claws so they stay in tact, remove the shell from the tail and cut into chunks, place all the lobster meat into the juices of the cooked shrimp and scallops on the sheet pan.
3. Place a knob of butter and a good drizzle of olive oil into the bottom of the risotto pot.
4. Add shallots and cook until they soften.
5. Add rice, stirring until coated and hot.
6. Deglaze with the Prosecco or white wine.
7. When liquid is absorbed then start adding your simmering warm seafood stock, one ladle at a time, stirring until it gets absorbed, then add another ladle full.
8. Keep flame on medium heat and continue adding warm stock and stirring until absorbed and rice reaches a tender and slightly al dente bite, you'll know when it's ready.
9. Turn off heat, add another knob of butter, a little olive oil, the drained chopped tomatoes and parsley, then stir to incorporate and finally add in your chopped seafood.
10. Put the lid on and let it rest for 1 minute.
11. When plating top each plate with one claw, garnish with more parsley

Drunken Risotto with Spinach

Ingredients:

3 cups dry red wine
2 cups chicken stock
2 tbsps. extra-virgin olive oil
3/4 pound bulk Italian sweet or hot sausage
1 small onion, finely chopped
2 large cloves garlic, finely chopped
1 1/2 cups arborio rice
Salt and pepper to taste
1/3 pound spinach leaves, stemmed and chopped (about 2 cups)
1/8 tsp. freshly grated nutmeg
2 tbsps. butter
1/2 cup grated pecorino-romano cheese

Directions:

1. In a large saucepan, combine the wine and chicken stock; keep warm over a low flame.
2. In a large, heavy pot, heat the olive oil, 2 turns of the pan, over medium-high heat.
3. Add the sausage and cook, crumbling the meat, until browned, about 2 minutes.
4. Add the onion and garlic and cook until softened, about 2 minutes.
5. Stir in the rice and season with salt and pepper.
6. Add the warm wine-stock mixture a couple of ladlefuls at a time, stirring vigorously after each addition and letting the liquid evaporate before adding more, cooking the risotto for 18 minutes.
7. In the last 5 minutes of cooking, stir in the spinach, a handful at a time, to wilt.
8. Stir in the nutmeg. In the last minute of cooking, stir in the butter, then the cheese.

Black Squid Ink Risotto

Risotto Ingredients:

2 tbsp butter
2 tbsp olive oil
1 medium shallot, diced
3 garlic cloves, minced
1 cup arborio rice
1/3 cup dry white wine
1 tsp squid ink, or more for a richer color
3 cups seafood stock or vegetable stock
salt and pepper, to taste

Scallops Ingredients:

1 /1/2 lbs. sea scallops, rinsed and dried
2 tsp unsalted butter
2 tsp olive oil
salt and pepper, to taste
fried sage leaves for garnish (optional)

Directions:

1. In a medium saucepan, bring the seafood stock to a simmer over medium-high heat, then reduce the heat to low to keep warm.
2. Heat the butter and olive oil over medium-high heat in a dutch oven or large sauté pan.
3. Add the chopped shallot and garlic and sauté for 1 to 2 minutes.
4. Add the arborio rice to the pan and stir to coat with butter (add more butter if every grain is not coated).
5. Cook the rice until it becomes translucent with an opaque center, about 2 minutes.
6. Deglaze the pan with the white wine. Allow the wine to simmer until it has completely reduced.
7. Stir in 1 tsp. of squid ink. Ladle about ½ cup to 1 cup of the hot seafood stock into the saucepan at a time, allowing the rice to completely absorb the liquid before adding another ladle.
8. Stir almost constantly.
9. After about 15 minutes, start tasting the rice for doneness. The rice should be served al dente - with just a little bit of bite. When the rice is almost done, add additional squid ink for a richer color, if desired. Salt and pepper to taste and serve with the seared scallops.
10. To Sear the Scallops:
11. Start preparing the scallops about 5 minutes before the risotto is done cooking.
12. Add the butter and oil to a sauté pan over high heat.
13. Season the scallops with salt and pepper, to taste.

14. Once the butter mixture begins to smoke, gently add the scallops, making sure there is ample room between the scallops. Sear each scallop for 1½ minutes per side, or until the scallops have developed a golden-brown crust but remain translucent in the center. Serve immediately with about 1 cup of squid ink risotto.

Creamy Maple Bacon Pumpkin Risotto

Ingredients:

4 thick slices bacon, diced
2 cups apple cider or juice (not spiced)
4 cups chicken or vegetable stock
1 1/2 cup leeks white and green part only, diced
4 garlic cloves, minced
2 cups Arborio rice
1 cup dry white wine
1/4 tsp. freshly grated nutmeg
1 tsp. sea salt
1/2 tsp. ground black pepper
1 1/2 cup pumpkin puree (fresh or canned, not pumpkin pie filling)
2 tbsps. pure maple syrup
Italian flat leaf parsley

Directions:

1. In a medium saucepan combine the chicken or vegetable stock and apple cider and set over very low heat.
2. In a stock pot or deep sided sauté pan cook the bacon over medium heat until crispy, about 10 minutes, being careful not to burn.
3. Remove with a slotted spoon to paper towels to drain.
4. Drain off all but 2 tbsp of the bacon fat and add the leeks and sauté until caramelized, about 8 minutes.
5. Add in the garlic and nutmeg and sauté until fragrant, another 30 seconds.
6. Add in the rice and the wine and stir well until the wine is cooked down. Turn the heat under the chicken stock to medium.
7. Add in ½ cup of chicken stock mixture to the rice mixture and stir until absorbed.
8. Repeat with ½ a cup at a time until the rice is al-dente, stirring well after each addition. You may not end up using all the chicken stock mixture.
9. Mix in the pumpkin puree and maple syrup and stir. Taste and season with salt and pepper. If the rice is chewier than desired add more chicken stock in and stir.
10. Stir in the bacon and serve immediately. Top with chopped Italian parsley and a little grated parmesan cheese.

Bacon, Cheddar & Beer Risotto

Ingredients:

1 tbsp. light butter
1/2 small onion, chopped
2 garlic cloves, minced
2 cups uncooked Arborio rice
12 oz. bottle of beer
6 cups chicken broth
1 1/2 oz. Parmesan cheese, freshly grated
3/4 cup sharp shredded cheddar cheese
2/3 cup shredded cheddar cheese
4 slices cooked extra lean turkey bacon
1/4 tsp. cayenne pepper

Directions:

1. Place the butter in a large sauté pan and bring it over medium-low heat until butter is just melted.
2. Add onions and cook 3-5 minutes until the onions are translucent.
3. Add the garlic and cook for another minute until garlic is fragrant.
4. Add the rice and stir to combine.
5. Cook an additional 2 minutes, stirring throughout.
6. Pour in the beer and turn the heat up to high until the beer begins to simmer.
7. Reduce heat back to medium-low and add ½ cup of the chicken broth.
8. Stir until the liquid dissolves and then add another ½ cup.
9. Repeat until all the broth has been added and the rice is creamy and al dente.
10. Remove the rice mixture from the heat and add the cheeses, bacon and cayenne pepper.
11. Stir until thoroughly combined and serve.

Red Wine Risotto

Ingredients:

32 oz. of chicken broth
20 oz. package of sweet Italian sausage
8 oz. baby bella mushrooms chopped small
1 cup arborio rice
1 cup red wine

Directions:

1. Heat the chicken broth over low heat. You could either use chicken broth by the can or box, or buy a small jar of broth base and add it to four cups of boiling water, turning the heat to a low simmer once it is combined. I prefer to use the base because it is much less expensive and I find myself using chicken broth so often.
2. Over medium high heat, remove the sausage from the casing and cook it in an oiled pan. (I like to just coat the inside of the pan in a spray of olive oil.) Season lightly with salt and pepper. Break it up as it cooks, stirring every few minutes until it is just cooked through, approximately 8 minutes.
3. Add the chopped mushrooms and cook until they are softened, approximately 3 minutes.
4. Turn the heat down to medium low.
5. Add the arborio rice, and stir. The rice will quickly soak up the cooking liquid from the sausage and the mushrooms.
6. Once there is minimal liquid left in the pan, add the wine, continuing to stir occasionally, approximately 6 minutes.
7. After the wine is absorbed, add the warm chicken broth one cup at a time until it is absorbed and the risotto is tender, approximately 15 minutes.

Caprese Risotto

Ingredients:

2 tbsps. olive oil, & then some for drizzling
2 cloves of garlic, minced
4 cups of chicken or vegetable broth
1 1/2 cups of arborio rice
1/2 cup white wine (optional)
1 tbsp. butter
2/3 cup shredded mozzarella cheese
Fresh basil leaves
Grape or cherry tomatoes

Directions:

1. Pour the chicken broth into a large saucepan. Over medium-low heat, start to slowly heat the broth to a low simmer.
2. Heat the 2 tbsp of olive oil over medium heat in a large dutch oven. Then add in the garlic and saute for a quick minute or two.
3. Add the cup of arborio rice to the garlic. Saute for another 1-2 minutes to slightly toast the rice.
4. Pour in your white wine now if you are choosing to add this.
5. Cook and stir the rice/wine mixture over medium heat until all the liquid is absorbed.
6. If you are skipping the wine in this dish, then just move on to the next step below.
7. Using a ladle, scoop in one ladle full of the chicken broth.
8. Cook and stir over medium-low heat until all the liquid is once again absorbed.
9. Continue doing this- ladling in the broth, stirring until absorbed until you have used all the chicken broth. This entire process should take between 30-35 minutes.
10. Once your risotto has absorbed all the liquid, remove from the heat and stir in the shredded mozzarella cheese and butter.
11. Season with salt and pepper to taste.
12. Top with fresh grape or cherry tomatoes and basil leaf chiffonades.
13. Finish each plate with a little drizzle of olive oil and enjoy!

Broccoli Cheddar Risotto

Ingredients:

4 cups chicken or vegetable stock
2 tbsps. olive oil
6 slices bacon, minced
1 medium onion, diced
1 cup Arborio rice
1 1/2 tbsps. lemon juice mixed with 2 1/2 tbsps. water
2 large cloves garlic, minced
2 cups broccoli florets, chopped small
1/8 tsp. black pepper
3 oz sharp cheddar, grated
2 tbsps. minced fresh parsley leaves, or any fresh herb you like (optional; for garnish)

Directions:

1. Bring chicken stock to a simmer in a medium saucepan over medium heat; turn heat down to low so it stays hot as you cook the risotto.
2. Heat the oil in a separate medium saucepan over medium heat; add the turkey bacon and cook until crispy, about 5 minutes. Remove the turkey bacon with a slotted spoon and set aside for now. Add the onion to the oil you cooked the turkey bacon in and cook until soft but not brown, about 5 minutes, stirring occasionally.
3. Add the rice and cook until slightly browned and nutty smelling, about 3 to 4 minutes, stirring occasionally. Add the lemon juice/water mixture and cook until evaporated, about 1 minute. Stir in the garlic, broccoli, and black pepper.
4. Turn heat down to medium-low. Add 1/2 cup of the hot stock to the rice, stirring constantly until the liquid is almost completely absorbed, then adding more stock in the same manner.
5. Continue this way until the risotto is tender with just a slight bite to it, about 20 to 25 minutes. (You may need slightly more or less liquid to achieve this; if you run out of stock, you can just simmer some water.)
6. Turn off heat and stir in the cheese and turkey bacon; add salt and pepper to taste. Sprinkle parsley on top (if using) and serve immediately.

Spinach Basil Pesto Risotto

Pesto Ingredients:

2 cloves Garlic
2 cups Packed Basil Leaves
1 cup Spinach Leaves
1/4 cup Olive Oil
3 Tbsps. Fresh Lemon Juice
Kosher Salt

Tomatoes Ingredients:

2 cups Cherry Tomatoes
2 Tbsps. Olive Oil
Kosher Salt

Risotto Ingredients:

4 Tbsps. Olive Oil
1/2 Yellow Onion, Diced Small
1 1/2 cup Arborio Rice
1 cup Dry White Wine
5 cups Vegetable Or Chicken Stock
Kosher Salt
Fresh Basil, For Garnish

Directions:

1. Preheat oven to 400 degrees F.
2. To make the pesto, combine garlic, basil, spinach, olive oil and lemon juice in the jar of a blender. Puree until smooth and then season with kosher salt. Set aside.
3. Place cherry tomatoes on a sheet pan prepared with a sheet of parchment paper. Drizzle with the olive oil and sprinkle with kosher salt.
4. Place in the oven and roast for 15 minutes.
5. For the risotto, in a large pan over medium heat, add the olive oil and onion. Saute the onion, stirring often, about 5 minutes.
6. Add rice and stir to coat the rice with the onion and oil.
7. Cook, stirring often, for 2 minutes.
8. Meanwhile, bring stock to a simmer over low heat in a small pot near by the pan.
9. Add wine to rice and stir, scraping any bits from the bottom of the pan. As the wine cooks off, add a large ladle of stock and continue to cook and stir. As the stock cooks off, add another ladle of stock. Continue this process of adding stock and cooking it off, stirring continuously.
10. When you are about 20 minutes in and have added most of the stock, add the spinach-basil pesto and the rest of the broth. Continue to cook another 2 minutes or until rice is tender and cooked through.
11. Season to taste with kosher salt.

12. Spoon into serving bowls and top with the roasted cherry tomatoes and a drizzle of olive oil. Garnish with fresh basil if desired.

Crispy Mozzarella Risotto Cakes

Ingredients:

1 1/2 cups leftover cold risotto
6 1/2-in. cubes mozzarella
1/3 cup vegetable oil

Directions:

1. Scoop about 1/4 cup risotto into palm of hand. Flatten slightly and press 1 cube of cheese (or 1 tsp goat cheese) into centre. Shape risotto into a ball around cheese.
2. Roll ball in panko, then place on a baking sheet.
3. Repeat with remaining rice, cheese and panko.
4. Heat a large frying pan over medium high.
5. Pour enough oil to come to 1/2 in. up the side, about 1/3 cup. When oil is hot, carefully place risotto balls into the pan and flatten slightly. (Do not crowd pan.
6. Cook in 2 batches if necessary.) Fry until golden, 3 to 4 min per side.
7. Remove to a paper-towel-lined plate.

Seafood Risotto

Ingredients:

1 cooked whole lobster, claws and tail, diced
8 shrimp, cooked peeled and deveined, diced
6 large scallops, cooked and diced
1 1/2 quart of seafood stock
cup arborio rice
2 large shallots
3/4 cup of Prosecco or white wine
1 cup of canned or fresh diced tomatoes, drained of wet liquid
Parsley
Olive oil and butter

Directions:

1. Cook the shrimp and scallops on a foil lined sheet pan, drizzle seafood with some garlic infused olive oil and a small handful of chopped parsley, roast at 425 degrees until pink and translucent, maybe 10 minutes, let it rest.
2. Break down your whole lobster tail, removing the shell from the claws so they stay in tact, remove the shell from the tail and cut into chunks, place all the lobster meat into the juices of the cooked shrimp and scallops on the sheet pan.
3. Place a knob of butter and a good drizzle of olive oil into the bottom of the risotto pot.
4. Add shallots and cook until they soften.
5. Add rice, stirring until coated and hot.
6. Deglaze with the Prosecco or white wine.
7. When liquid is absorbed then start adding your simmering warm seafood stock, one ladle at a time, stirring until it gets absorbed, then add another ladle full.
8. Keep flame on medium heat and continue adding warm stock and stirring until absorbed and rice reaches a tender and slightly al dente bite, you'll know when it's ready.
9. Turn off heat, add another knob of butter, a little olive oil, the drained chopped tomatoes and parsley, then stir to incorporate and finally add in your chopped seafood.
10. Put the lid on and let it rest for 1 minute.
11. When plating top each plate with one claw, garnish with more parsley

Drunken Risotto with Spinach

Ingredients:

3 cups dry red wine
2 cups chicken stock
2 tbsps. extra-virgin olive oil
3/4 pound bulk Italian sweet or hot sausage
1 small onion, finely chopped
2 large cloves garlic, finely chopped
1 1/2 cups arborio rice
Salt and pepper to taste
1/3 pound spinach leaves, stemmed and chopped (about 2 cups)
1/8 tsp. freshly grated nutmeg
2 tbsps. butter
1/2 cup grated pecorino-romano cheese

Directions:

1. In a large saucepan, combine the wine and chicken stock; keep warm over a low flame.
2. In a large, heavy pot, heat the olive oil, 2 turns of the pan, over medium-high heat.
3. Add the sausage and cook, crumbling the meat, until browned, about 2 minutes.
4. Add the onion and garlic and cook until softened, about 2 minutes.
5. Stir in the rice and season with salt and pepper.
6. Add the warm wine-stock mixture a couple of ladlefuls at a time, stirring vigorously after each addition and letting the liquid evaporate before adding more, cooking the risotto for 18 minutes.
7. In the last 5 minutes of cooking, stir in the spinach, a handful at a time, to wilt.
8. Stir in the nutmeg. In the last minute of cooking, stir in the butter, then the cheese.

Black Squid Ink Risotto

Risotto Ingredients:

2 tbsp butter
2 tbsp olive oil
1 medium shallot, diced
3 garlic cloves, minced
1 cup arborio rice
1/3 cup dry white wine
1 tsp squid ink, or more for a richer color
3 cups seafood stock or vegetable stock
salt and pepper, to taste

Scallops Ingredients:

1 /1/2 lbs. sea scallops, rinsed and dried
2 tsp unsalted butter
2 tsp olive oil
salt and pepper, to taste
fried sage leaves for garnish (optional)

Directions:

1. In a medium saucepan, bring the seafood stock to a simmer over medium-high heat, then reduce the heat to low to keep warm.
2. Heat the butter and olive oil over medium-high heat in a Dutch oven or large sauté pan.
3. Add the chopped shallot and garlic and sauté for 1 to 2 minutes.
4. Add the arborio rice to the pan and stir to coat with butter (add more butter if every grain is not coated).
5. Cook the rice until it becomes translucent with an opaque center, about 2 minutes.
6. Deglaze the pan with the white wine.
7. Allow the wine to simmer until it has completely reduced.
8. Stir in 1 tsp. of squid ink. Ladle about ½ cup to 1 cup of the hot seafood stock into the saucepan at a time, allowing the rice to completely absorb the liquid before adding another ladle.
9. Stir almost constantly.
10. After about 15 minutes, start tasting the rice for doneness. The rice should be served al dente - with just a little bit of bite.
11. When the rice is almost done, add additional squid ink for a richer color, if desired. Salt and pepper to taste and serve with the seared scallops.
12. To Sear the Scallops:
13. Start preparing the scallops about 5 minutes before the risotto is done cooking.
14. Add the butter and oil to a sauté pan over high heat.
15. Season the scallops with salt and pepper, to taste.

16. Once the butter mixture begins to smoke, gently add the scallops, making sure there is ample room between the scallops.
17. Sear each scallop for 1 1/2 minutes per side, or until the scallops have developed a golden-brown crust but remain translucent in the center. Serve immediately with about 1 cup of squid ink risotto.

About the Author

Laura Sommers is **The Recipe Lady!**

She is a loving wife and mother who lives on a small farm in Baltimore County, Maryland and has a passion for all things domestic especially when it comes to saving money. She has a profitable eBay business and is a couponing addict. Follow her tips and tricks to learn how to make delicious meals on a budget, save money or to learn the latest life hack!

Visit her Amazon Author Page to see her latest books:

amazon.com/author/laurasommers

Visit the Recipe Lady's blog for even more great recipes:

http://the-recipe-lady.blogspot.com/

Follow the Recipe Lady on **Pinterest**:

http://pinterest.com/therecipelady1

Other Books by Laura Sommers

- Recipe Hacks for Beer
- Recipe Hacks for Potato Chips
- Recipe Hacks for a Bottle of Italian Salad Dressing
- Recipe Hacks for Dry Onion Soup Mix
- Recipe Hacks for Cheese Puffs
- Recipe Hacks for Pasta Sauce
- Recipe Hacks for Dry Vegetable Soup Mix
- Recipe Hacks for Canned Tuna Fish
- Recipe Hacks for Saltine Crackers
- Recipe Hacks for Pancake Mix
- Recipe Hacks for Instant Mashed Potato Flakes
- Recipe Hacks for Sriracha Hot Chili Sauce
- Recipe Hacks for Dry Ranch Salad Dressing and Dip Mix
- Recipe Hacks for Canned Biscuits
- Recipe Hacks for Canned Soup
- Recipe Hacks for Oreo Cookies
- Recipe Hacks for a Box of Mac & Cheese

Printed in Great Britain
by Amazon